KIRBY Puckett

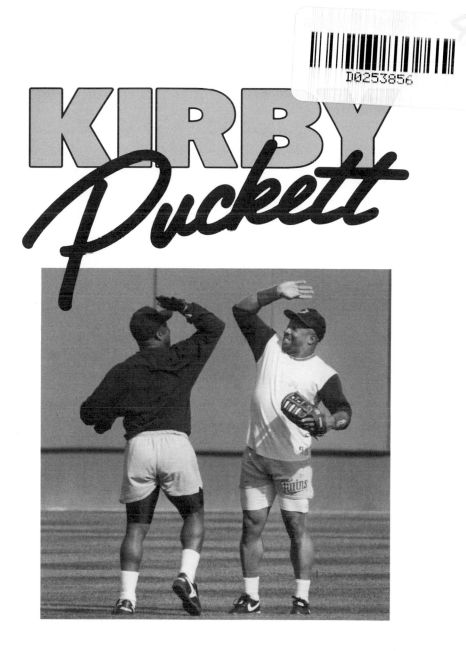

KIRBY Puckett

Fan Favorite

Ann Bauleke

Lerner Publications Company ■ Minneapolis

ACKNOWLEDGMENTS

Photographs are reproduced with the permission of: St. Paul Pioneer Press, pp. 1 and 8 (Joe Rossi), pp. 2 and 11 (Richard Marshall), p. 6 (Buzz Magnuson), and pp. 55 and 61 (Jean Pieri); Rick Orndorf/Minnesota Twins, pp. 9, 19, 20, 46, 48, 54, 57, 58, 62; Chicago Housing Authority, p. 12; Chicago White Sox, p. 15; Bradley University, p. 24; Triton College Athletic Department, pp. 25, 26; Elizabethton Newspapers Inc., p. 27; Visalia Times-Delta, p. 28; Minnesota Twins, pp. 33, 35, 38, 41, 42, 45, 51; Star Tribune/Minneapolis-St. Paul, pp. 37 (© 1986) and 52 (© 1992); and Mitchell B. Reibel/SportsChrome East/West, p. 49. Front and back cover photographs of Kirby Puckett are reproduced by permission of Rick Orndorf/Minnesota Twins. Cover photograph of crowd is courtesy of the Minnesota Twins.

This book is available in two editions:
Library binding by Lerner Publications Company
Soft cover by First Avenue Editions
241 First Avenue North, Minneapolis, Minnesota 55401

Information in this book came from the author's many interviews with Kirby Puckett for her baseball column in a weekly Twin Cities newspaper. Other information is from the following sources: *Sport, Sports Illustrated, The Sporting News, Baseball Card News, Star Tribune of the Twin Cities, St. Paul Pioneer Press, Minnesota Calls,* and *Twins Magazine.*

Library of Congress Cataloging-in-Publication Data

Bauleke, Ann.
  Kirby Puckett : fan favorite / Ann Bauleke.
    p.   cm. — (The Achievers)
  Summary: Profiles the personality, childhood, and career of the popular Minnesota Twins outfielder.
  ISBN 0-8225-0490-1
    1. Puckett, Kirby—Juvenile literature. 2. Baseball players—United States—Biography—Juvenile literature. 3. Minnesota Twins (Baseball team)—Juvenile literature. [1. Puckett, Kirby. 2. Baseball players.] I. Title. II. Series.
GV865.P83B38   1993
796.357'092—dc20
[B]   92-15271
                                                                          CIP
                                                                           AC

Manufactured in the United States of America

International Standard Book Number: 0-8225-0490-1 (lib. bdg.)
International Standard Book Number: 0-8225-9633-4 (pbk.)
Library of Congress Catalog Card Number: 92-15271

2   3   4   5   6   98   97   96   95   94   93

Contents

Cameras and microphones record Kirby's celebration with team-mate Chili Davis after game seven of the 1991 World Series.

1

Game Six

All season, day after day, Kirby Puckett is one of the first of the Minnesota Twins on the field for extra batting practice. Now, hours before the start of game six of the 1991 World Series, he enters the dugout. The seats inside the Metrodome are empty and the grounds crew is touching up the red, white, and blue World Series logo painted on the turf. As Kirby slides his bats into the bat rack, their barrels roll together, making a wooden clang. He chooses one for batting practice. "Don't worry," Kirby tells his teammates. "I'll carry everybody tonight."

The Minnesota Twins and the Atlanta Braves are back in the Metrodome to resume their improbable, suspenseful World Series. The Twins won the first two games at home, but when the teams played in Atlanta, the Twins lost three in a row. Minnesota needs to win tonight just to keep its Series hopes alive.

So far in the World Series, Kirby has only three hits in 18 at bats. He and the Twins will be facing Steve Avery, one of the youngest but toughest left-handed pitchers in major league baseball.

When the game starts, the Twins waste no time. With one out in the bottom of the first inning, rookie Chuck Knoblauch singles. Kirby follows with a hit that hugs the left-field line and travels all the way to the corner. By the time Kirby slides into third base with a triple, Knoblauch has scored the Twins' first run. The hit brings the 55,000-plus fans to their feet, wildly waving Homer Hankies. Kirby scores on a single by Shane Mack, and the Twins have a quick 2-0 lead.

Kirby comes up with the ball that Ron Gant sent deep into center field.

The scoreboard message reflects what thousands of fans are thinking.

In the third inning, Kirby saves a run on defense. Running all the way back to the center-field wall, he jumps and puts his glove against the plexiglass to snare Ron Gant's long shot. The fantastic catch prevents Atlanta from scoring and protects the Minnesota lead. Kirby doesn't have a chance to stop Terry Pendleton's two-run homer in the fifth inning, however, and the Braves tie the game. In the Twins' half of the fifth inning, Kirby helps the Twins regain the lead, scoring Dan Gladden from third base on a sacrifice fly.

Atlanta ties the game again in the seventh inning. For three more innings—into extra innings—the teams battle, but no one scores.

In the bottom of the 11th inning, with the Twins due to bat, raw nerves stir activity in the Twins' dugout. One player grabs a bag of sunflower seeds; another strolls to the water fountain. Players on the bench lean forward, resting their elbows on their knees. The attention is on Kirby. He'll be the first batter up.

To the surprise of Twins fans, Braves manager Bobby Cox brings lefthander Charlie Liebrandt in to pitch. Liebrandt lost to the Twins in game one. In fact, the Twins have a history of hitting well against Liebrandt, who had faced them often as a member of the Kansas City Royals in the American League. Also, Kirby has always hit best against lefties.

In the on-deck circle, Kirby and designated hitter Chili Davis watch Liebrandt warm up. Kirby's a hacker. He can hit almost any pitch. Sometimes, though, he looks silly swinging at a ball far out of the strike zone. The Braves have been getting him out on pitches low and outside. "Do me a favor," Chili tells Kirby. "Don't swing at anything low." Kirby promises, but Chili laughs. Kirby is likely to swing at anything.

Finally, Liebrandt takes his final warm-up pitch. Kirby walks up to the plate. The crowd is waving Homer Hankies and cheering, "Kirrr-bee, Kirrr-bee!"

Kirby rounds the bases after his game-winning homer.

 With two balls and a strike on him, Kirby swings at the fourth pitch. The bat meets the ball just right. In left and center, the fielders run back, back. But the ball keeps soaring, right over the plexiglass at the top of the wall. As Kirby rounds first base, the ball lands in the stands. The Twins win. The Series will continue for one more game. As Kirby runs the bases, he pumps his fist. He yells out loud, "Yeh! Yeh!" Sprinting out of the dugout, Kirby's teammates holler too.

The Pucketts lived in this housing project, where kids played on asphalt playgrounds. The projects were home to many poor families, who lived in huge 16-story buildings like the one in the background.

2
Escape from the Projects

In Chicago, Illinois, not far from Lake Michigan on the south side of the city, the White Sox play baseball. Until their new ballpark opened across the street in 1991, the Sox played at old Comiskey Park, which was about nine blocks away from where Kirby Puckett grew up. Kirby's family lived in a housing project named the Robert Taylor Homes. Many kids who lived in the projects belonged to gangs. They sold drugs, stole things, and got into knife fights. They painted the names and symbols of their gangs on the walls of the apartment lobby. Once, when Kirby was a child, a student brought a machine gun to school and shot at teachers and the principal. Kirby never ran home so fast as he did that day.

But that same elementary school rewarded good students with tickets to baseball games. Watching his baseball idols was Kirby's greatest thrill. "I had a smile on my face for 24 hours," Kirby recalls, "just knowing I went to the game and actually saw these guys play."

In a family of nine children—three girls and six boys—Kirby is the youngest. He was born March 14, 1961, six years after the Pucketts' next youngest son. The Pucketts lived on the 14th floor of a 16-story building. Most of the time, the elevator didn't work. Kirby walked up and down the stairs with his bat, glove, and ball. "Nobody bothered me," Kirby recalls. "They'd say, 'There's Kirby. He just wants to play baseball.'"

There was no green, grassy yard around the projects. Kirby played on asphalt and rock-hard dirt enclosed within the walls of four buildings. He played a game called "strikeout." On one wall, the kids drew a square as high as a kid's chest and as low as his knees to represent a strike zone. Throwing a small rubber ball, the pitcher aimed for the square on the wall. If the hitter didn't swing and the ball hit the square, the pitch was a strike. Three strikes counted as an out, just like in regular baseball. Each batter got three outs. When the ball hit the wall, it bounced back toward the pitcher, which made a catcher unnecessary. There were seldom enough players to field an entire team anyway, because so few kids wanted to play.

Balls hit to the outfield bounced off the opposite wall. If a ball hit the wall without touching the ground, it was a home run. If it hit after one bounce, it was scored a triple. Two bounces counted as a double, and three or more as a single. There was one more rule: If the ball broke a window—everybody ran away! Kirby remembers breaking a window in a third-floor apartment and running home. About five minutes later, a neighbor knocked on the door, complaining about the broken window.

"I never could lie to my mom," Kirby recalls. "She wouldn't punish me or anything [for a broken window], she'd just make me earn the money to pay for that window."

Comiskey Park was nine blocks from the Pucketts' home, across a major highway.

Kirby's mother, Catherine Puckett, was the disciplinarian in the family. She wanted her kids to learn to be responsible. Even though she allowed Kirby to play outside all day long, he still had rules to obey. At night, by the time the street lights came on, she expected him home. She also expected him to avoid troublemakers. "Don't go over there," she warned him. Sometimes Kirby's curiosity tempted him, though. "I was the kind of kid who said, 'I'll see for myself.' So I'd sneak over there," Kirby recalls. "They'd be drinking or whatever, selling drugs. Probably stealing. If kids your age had all this money—20, 30 dollars— you knew something wasn't right. I'd go, 'Well, my mom was right. There's nothing over there but trouble.'

"Most of the people I grew up with are either dead or in jail," Kirby says. "People were always getting beaten up and shot. I knew you didn't get that playing baseball."

Kirby's father worked two jobs, and his workweek ended Saturday at noon. On Saturday and Sunday, Bill Puckett liked to sit in his chair. He was a gentle, soft-hearted man. When Catherine scolded the kids, they sought comfort from their dad. But Bill would not be fooled. When the kids tried to cuddle up to him for sympathy, he simply said, "Now you know what you did was wrong."

In the Puckett home, learning to be responsible included learning to manage money. The Pucketts were poor, but not as poor as most of the families in the Robert Taylor Homes. Kirby's mother clipped discount coupons from the newspaper. She knew how to stretch a dollar. Kirby didn't ask for much. As long as he had a bat, a ball, and a glove, he was happy.

When he needed a new glove, he just let his dad know. A day or two later the glove appeared. Perhaps buying his son gloves and baseballs was Bill's way of encouraging Kirby to continue the sport. Kirby's father had played baseball for an all-black team before baseball was integrated—that is, before black players were allowed to play on the same team as white players. However, Bill Puckett never talked to Kirby about the experience.

Kirby's parents gave him $12 each week for expenses such as lunch and bus fare to and from school. The allowance helped teach responsibility, and Kirby was soon a shrewd manager of money. Each week he laid out his allowance on his bed. He figured $12 provided almost $2.50 a day for the five weekdays. He calculated his daily expenses, then figured out how much extra money he would have for other things, like a can of soda after school.

Kirby must have been lonely. Few kids his age were interested in baseball. Some kids didn't like to play with him because he was too good. By the time he was 10, Kirby was playing baseball with 16-year-olds. They were a better match for his talent.

Sometimes he bought candy with part of his allowance and bribed other kids into playing with him. "Like if I had a dollar," Kirby explains, "I'd buy 100 pieces of candy. [But] when all the candy was gone, I'd have nothing to maneuver them with. So they'd go their way and I'd end up playing by myself. Nobody liked to hang around with me because I played baseball all the time."

Girls, however, almost always liked Kirby. "Not because I played baseball," Kirby says. "They just liked me." Even his mother found it difficult to understand. "What do they see in your ugly self?" she teased him. The girls were welcomed into the Puckett home, where they often watched TV with Kirby. Catherine served them Kool Aid and buttered popcorn.

When Kirby was 12, the family moved to a new apartment. The postal service had promoted Bill, allowing the family to move out of the projects and into a better neighborhood. "It was heaven to me," Kirby recalls. Instead of a 16-floor apartment building with a broken elevator, they lived in a two-story building. "There were white folks who lived on the floor below us, and white people next door," Kirby says. "I got a chance to go out and experience the other parts of living. The white kids accepted me. I didn't bother nobody. I found out where the park was and went about my business." He had his bicycle, his bat, his ball, and his glove. "I went to the park and played ball by myself. If someone else came over [and said,] 'Can I play with you?'—you know how kids are—I said, 'Sure.'"

Kirby was always short. His brothers and sisters resembled their tall and lean father, but Kirby took after his mother. "This build you see now," Kirby says, "it's just like my mom. She had broad shoulders, and she had *calves*. My feet are identical to hers. My smile. I got my mom's nose."

Kirby says he resembles his mother.

Kirby's muscles are stacked from his legs to his neck. In high school, he decided that if he was going to be short, at least he would be strong. At a time when bodybuilder Arnold Schwartzenegger was very popular, Kirby and a friend embarked on a body-building regimen. Every morning before school, they gulped drinks made of raw eggs and orange juice. They began a strict weight-lifting program. Before long, Kirby's body had become stocky.

When football began to seem attractive to Kirby, his mother wouldn't allow him to play. The risk of injury in football was too great, she said. Catherine Puckett believed that Kirby could play major league baseball someday.

On the base paths, Kirby has the speed of a fullback, but he never played organized football.

Kirby attended Calumet High School in a rough neighborhood of south Chicago. Scouts from college baseball teams avoided traveling into the neighborhood. They preferred to search for talented athletes at schools located in safer areas around Chicago. If Kirby was going to attract any attention from these scouts, he would have to play well when his team played at other schools.

Kirby wanted to attend college so he could continue to develop as a baseball player. He also wanted an education, in case he never realized his dream of playing professional baseball. When he finally received a scholarship offer from Miami Dade North Junior College in Florida, however, he turned it down. "I decided I wanted to take a year off from school and baseball and see what else was out there," he says. "This was the one year that was really experimental for me."

Kirby was 18 when he started his first job, installing carpet in new cars at Ford Motor Company. He jumped at the chance to earn $8 an hour when all his friends worked at fast-food restaurants, earning only the minimum wage. "Grab the carpet," he says, describing his work, "[and] throw it in. For the carpet to be just right, we had to get it down with the bolts so the guys could put the seats in. I was sore for the first couple of weeks from lifting all that carpet." But the pay was good.

Kirby stopped on his way home from work to cash his first paycheck— $500. At home he laid the money out on his bed. Then he called his parents into his bedroom. "I want you to take whatever you want and enjoy yourselves," he told them. "They didn't want to take anything," Kirby recalls. "They took like $100 or something." He deposited the rest of the money into a bank account.

Kirby worked at Ford for almost three months. Then, a day before he would join the labor union and earn an even higher wage, he was fired. According to company rules, employees had to work three months before they could join the union. Instead of paying Kirby more money, Ford hired someone new at the cheaper wage.

With the help of a friend, Kirby found another job filing registration cards in alphabetical order for the United States Census Bureau. There he earned $6 an hour. In the meantime, Kirby still played baseball. He played for a semiprofessional team called the Pirates. Kirby also went to a tryout camp for the Kansas City Royals in 1980. There, a baseball coach from Bradley University in Peoria, Illinois, spotted him. After checking Kirby's grades, the coach offered him a scholarship to attend Bradley and play baseball. The scholarship would pay all of Kirby's college expenses.

Kirby said he'd have to talk it over with his parents.

3

The Road to the Major Leagues

When Catherine and Bill Puckett heard the news, they were proud. They had taken care of Kirby his whole life. Now it was time for him to take care of himself. "I was stepping out to be a man and take that responsibility. It wasn't going to be 'Well, Mom, I need money.' I was on my own. That's pretty scary.

"When I left for college—I'll never forget it as long as I live—my mom and dad were standing at the front door and tears were coming from their eyes. I was only going two hours away. But it was my time to go." That turned out to be the last time Kirby saw his father. Three weeks later, Bill Puckett suffered a heart attack and died.

Kirby wanted to quit school and take care of his mother, but she protested. "We've invested too many baseballs in you," she told him. Kirby finished the year at Bradley and played baseball in the spring. He batted .378, hit eight home runs (tying the school's single season record), and batted in 41 runs. He was named to the All-Missouri Valley Conference team. The year at Bradley was also the year Kirby switched positions. He had played third base, but his coach moved him to the outfield.

When classes ended in the spring of 1981, Kirby joined a summer collegiate baseball league. There, he attracted the attention of Jim Rantz, who was assistant director of the Minnesota Twins' farm system. Rantz's son Mike played in the same league, and Rantz found time to watch some games. That coincidence would prove to be fateful for Kirby.

Kirby played baseball for Bradley just one season, in 1981. It was there that his coach, Dewey Kalmer, switched him to center field.

Kirby takes a lead off second base during a 1982 game for Triton Junior College.

In the fall, Kirby attended Triton Junior College—just west of Chicago—in River Grove, Illinois, so he could be closer to home. Every night before bed, he called his mother. "I couldn't sleep unless I heard her voice," he says.

Midway through the school year, the Twins, at Rantz's urging, took Kirby with their first pick—the third overall—in the January 1982 draft. Kirby rejected the Twins' first offer, which included a $4,000 signing bonus. He decided to attend school for another semester and play junior college baseball in the spring.

Even after he was a major leaguer, Kirby returned to Triton and helped with a baseball camp for young ball players.

At Triton he excelled at baseball, but he was also serious about his education. When Kirby wasn't dreaming of hitting baseballs in the major leagues, he imagined becoming a police officer or a private investigator. He studied criminal justice to learn about the system of law and order. "Even the teacher told me I was one of the smartest guys," Kirby says. "I never drifted off in criminal justice class, because I wanted to know how the system works and how people actually go about getting around in the system."

In junior college baseball, Kirby batted .472 and hit 16 home runs. When he was named the Junior College Player of the Year in Triton's region, the Twins increased their offer and included a $20,000 signing bonus. This time, Kirby signed.

Kirby spent the 1982 season, his first year in professional baseball, with the Twins' rookie league team in Elizabethton, Tennessee. Hitting .382 in 65 games and stealing 43 bases, he earned a spot on the league's all-star team.

While Kirby launched his career with a burst of success, his major league parent club had its worst season in the team's history. It was the Twins' first season inside the new domed stadium in Minneapolis. The Metrodome is a gigantic construction with a Teflon roof for a sky and AstroTurf for grass. Angry fans refused to watch baseball indoors. To make matters worse, the young and inexperienced team finished last in its division, losing 102 games that season.

Kirby spent his first professional baseball season in the minor leagues with the Elizabethton Twins in Tennessee.

Kirby's success in Visalia, California, caught the attention of his major league club, the Minnesota Twins.

In 1983 Kirby moved to the next step in the minor leagues and played the season with the Twins' Class A team in Visalia, California. The Class A season is longer than the rookie league season, so Kirby played in 138 games. He ended up hitting .314 with 97 runs batted in (RBI) and 48 stolen bases. He was selected to the California League All-Star team and was named Player of the Year.

The major league Twins improved slightly in 1983, ending the season tied for fifth place. The team still lacked talent at some positions.

Kirby began the 1984 season in Class AAA (Triple A), the highest rung in the minor leagues. Within a month, however, he had reached his goal. He had been called up to the major leagues. His minor league team, the Toledo Mud Hens, were playing in Maine when Kirby got the call. The Twins were playing the California Angels on the other side of the United States. To get there, Kirby had to fly first from Maine to Atlanta, Georgia. Then he had to catch a connecting flight to Los Angeles, California. Kirby's flight from Maine to Atlanta went fine. In Atlanta, however, he and the other passengers had to wait several hours while mechanics repaired the plane that was to take them to Los Angeles.

The Twins had promised to send someone to meet Kirby at the Los Angeles airport, but when the plane finally landed, no one was waiting for him. To make matters worse, Kirby didn't have enough money with him to rent a car or to take a taxi to the Angels' stadium in Anaheim. Eventually, he convinced a taxi driver that he really was a ball player for the Minnesota Twins. He promised to leave his suitcase in the taxi while he searched the clubhouse for someone from the Twins' organization to pay the fare.

Despite Kirby's frantic efforts to get to the ballpark, he didn't arrive in time to play in that day's game. But Twins manager Billy Gardner put Kirby into the leadoff spot the next day, May 8. In his first at bat, Kirby fouled off several pitches. "I wonder if I'm going to be able to hit big league pitching," he said to himself. Kirby not only was able to hit the pitches, he got four hits in five times up during the game. He launched his major league career with a seven-game hitting streak.

4
Thriving in The Show

During his rookie year, Kirby didn't always feel as confident as he appeared. Everything but the baseballs was new to him. He had to make many adjustments. For instance, each ballpark around the major leagues is different from the next. The visitors' locker room is located in a different cranny of each stadium. In every city, he had new questions: Where do you find a good restaurant? How do you get around in the city?

Getting around is one small challenge. Getting along in major league baseball is another. The major leagues are a world of their own and very different from the life Kirby had known. Also, as he became more well-known, he had to adjust to being a public figure.

But Kirby was happy to be in the major leagues, and he accepted the responsibility that came with the opportunity. He quickly became most everyone's favorite. Kids loved him for the sound of his name, his 5-foot-8 size, and his cuddly shape. They liked Kirby even more because he took time to talk with them and sign autographs. Twins fans loved his hustle. Kirby worked hard to be the player people expected him to be.

Despite all the challenges of playing major league baseball, Kirby stayed upbeat. If he fell into a batting slump, he would tell reporters that he wasn't worried. If he just hit one ball well, he'd break out of the slump, he told them. "There are 162 games [each season], so you can't let yourself get too down if you lose. You have to handle the good and the bad," he said. "Sometimes it's hard to stay up if things aren't going well, but you have to do it."

Kirby found a friend in Twins infielder Ron Washington. Washington had spent most of 11 years in the minor leagues before 1982, his first full season in the big leagues. He shared what he had learned with everyone, especially the rookie, Kirby. "He took me under his wing," Kirby says, "and showed me what the big leagues were all about."

Washington helped the players stay relaxed, especially in tense situations when they wanted with all their hearts to be successful. "You will or you won't," Washington always said, "You do or you don't."

The Twins surprised themselves by winning more often than not in 1984. A few days after Kirby made his major league debut, the Twins were in first place. Kirby covered vast territory in center field. He played deep, toward the center-field wall. He was good at charging the ball and letting it drop into his glove. At the plate, he was a hacker, swinging at nearly every pitch, whether it was in the strike zone or not. First baseman Kent Hrbek, third baseman Gary Gaetti, and outfielder Tom Brunansky were power hitters. If Kirby got on base, the big guys behind him had the power to hit him home. As a result, the Twins might explode for a bunch of runs at any moment. They won thrilling games in the late innings.

Kirby (center) poses with (left to right) teammates Gary Gaetti, Tom Brunansky, Kent Hrbek, and Roy Smalley. In the mid-1980s, these players provided most of Minnesota's offensive power.

But they still had weak spots on the team. The starting pitching usually gave up a lot of runs early. The late-inning victories often occurred only after the Twins had fallen behind in the first three innings.

Ready or not, by September the Twins were in a race to win the American League West. Some people say the Twins choked. Some people say they just weren't experienced enough or talented enough to win. Whatever the reason, they faltered. In the last series of the 1984 season, the Twins lost to the Cleveland Indians. Meanwhile, the Kansas City Royals beat California to clinch the division title. Kirby ended his rookie season hitting .296. He scored 63 runs and batted in 31. He hit no home runs.

During the next season, 1985, Kirby began seeing a pattern he didn't like. He noticed that when he came up to bat, the other team's outfielders shifted. They took a few steps toward right field. After watching Kirby for a season, the other teams figured out that most of his hits landed in right and right-center field. The outfield shift placed the fielders a step or two closer to where Kirby usually hit the ball. As a result, balls that might have dropped for hits fell into the gloves of cagey outfielders instead.

Kirby was frustrated. Outfielders seldom shift on good hitters, because it doesn't do any good. Good hitters can hit to all fields—left, right, and center. Kirby wanted his hitting to command that kind of respect. He worked hard through the season, finishing with a .288 average. He hit four home runs. At the end of the 1985 season, Kirby and hitting coach Tony Oliva promised to work together in spring training the next year.

Tony Oliva (left), who was an excellent hitter during his playing career with the Twins, helped Kirby refine his approach to batting.

Oliva knew how to hit. During his 15-year playing career with the Twins, he won three batting titles and retired with a .304 batting average. He hoped to help Kirby improve his skill for pulling the ball. For a right-handed batter like Kirby, that meant hitting the ball to left field. Oliva believed that Kirby could hit more home runs if he practiced pulling the ball when he got a pitch on the inside part of the plate. As the Twins kept losing, Kirby continued to work to be the best player he could be.

During this same period of dedication to improving his game, Kirby was also enjoying his personal life in Minneapolis. He had met Tonya Hudson, and the two became engaged in the fall of 1985. Even though Kirby was one of the most popular players in Minnesota, Tonya had never heard of him before she met him. She didn't know very much about baseball. In fact, she was surprised to learn that Kirby would be away from Minnesota for a week or more at a time while he traveled with the team on road trips.

When the couple was married in November 1986, they moved into a large home that they hired carpenters to build especially for them. It was the first house Kirby had ever called home. "I've lived in a lot of apartments, but this is a *house...my* house," he said.

In the spring of 1986, Kirby came on like gangbusters. He had a seven-game hitting streak in April and was named American League Player of the Month.

Kirby and Tonya in front of their new house

For the first time in his career, he was named the starting center fielder for the American League in the All-Star game. He played the whole game, getting one hit, a walk, and a stolen base.

Kirby worked as though his best had yet to be discovered. He didn't wait for a winning team to make his work easier, just as he never waited to find friends to play with him when he was growing up. He always found a way to do what he wanted to do.

In 1986 the Twins ended up in sixth place out of the seven teams in their division. But Kirby hit 31 home runs and batted .328 with 96 RBI. His work with Oliva had paid off. He was the first player ever to hit no home runs in his first 500 at bats, then come back and hit at least 30 homers in a season. From then on, the Twins would expect Kirby to hit homers.

Kirby and Kent Hrbek greet teammate Randy Bush at home plate during the 1987 World Series.

5

From Chumps to Champs

In the early 1980s, people often called the young and inexperienced Twins the "Twinkies"—a nickname that had been used in previous losing seasons. Some players were offended, but Kirby never let it bother him. "People can say what they want," he said. "I'm in the big leagues now, so I'm not a Twinkie." However, the Twins were still trying to get the right players in the right positions so they could turn their luck around.

Before spring training in 1987, Twins management made several roster moves in an effort to strengthen the team. They traded with Montreal to get Jeff Reardon, a valuable closer (a pitcher whose job is to save a small lead late in the game). He had led the majors with 107 saves over the three previous years. Reardon joined a pitching staff that included starters Bert Blyleven and Frank Viola. Both Blyleven and

Viola had won more than 15 games for the Twins in 1986. Hrbek, Gaetti, Brunansky, and Kirby remained the core of the team. Greg Gagne had developed into a graceful shortstop, and the Twins had picked up Dan Gladden from the San Francisco Giants.

Late in the 1986 season the Twins hired their third base coach, Tom Kelly, to manage the team. Kelly had played, coached, and managed in the minor leagues for years. He knew how to use pitchers in a game, and where to place players in the lineup and on the field. And he knew about hard work. Together, he and Kirby set an example for the rest of the team.

In 1987 Kirby was widely recognized for leaping against the wall in center field to pluck home-run balls out of midair. Using a technique he had polished in previous seasons, he actually robbed hitters of home runs. Kirby chugged back, back, back. At the wall, he leaped high enough to snatch the ball just before it could clear the top. It was an amazing sight, as thrilling as if Kirby had hit a home run himself.

By the All-Star break, the Twins were in first place. They were still losing their share of games, but so were other teams in the division. Minnesota fans were so unprepared for a winner that they kept waiting for the Twins to cave in. The team never did.

Kirby was the starting center fielder in the All-Star game again in 1987. But in four at bats, he failed to get a hit. Kirby spent the month of July in a slump.

Kirby and Texas Ranger first baseman Pete O'Brien chat during
the game that eventually clinched a 1987 play-off spot for the
Twins.

Gary Gaetti and Kirby model Minnesota's new style of uniforms,
which the Twins wore for the first time during the 1987 season.

He had only four hits in 29 at bats. "Right now, I'm not swinging very well at all," Kirby said at the time. But he remained optimistic. "All I have to do is hit one ball good, and then I'll get started again. That's what usually gets me started. Hitting one ball hard seems to get my timing back." Hrbek, Gaetti, and Brunansky were having good years, and Kirby didn't coast. At night he took his bat home with him and swung it in the living room while he listened to music on the stereo.

With one week remaining in the 1987 season, the Twins clinched the division title. To many people, the Twins' success seemed too good to be true. The national media said that the Twins making the playoffs was a fluke, since they had won only 85 games that season. The Detroit Tigers, with a veteran pitching staff, were heavily favored to win the American League Championship Series and advance to the World Series.

The Twins adopted an underdog's attitude: "According to the 'experts,' we aren't supposed to be here. So we have nothing to lose." Then, to everyone's surprise, the Twins defeated the Tigers, four games to one. Kirby didn't have a particularly good series, however. He contributed only five hits in 24 at bats, including one home run. But the Twins won, and the fans were ecstatic. Waving their Homer Hankies, more than 55,000 fans turned the Metrodome into a magic kingdom. Next stop: the World Series, against the National League Champion St. Louis Cardinals. "We did it," Kirby said joyously after beating Detroit. "I can't believe it. Some guys play 10, 12, 20 years and never make it to the World Series. I'm going, and I've only played four. I might not do it again, but I'm here now and I'm going to enjoy it."

Like the Tigers, St. Louis boasted a fine pitching staff and experienced hitters. Again, the sportswriters pointed at the Twins' regular season record and said their luck wouldn't hold out. Nearly everyone predicted the Cardinals would win the World Series, but the Twins won the first two games in the Metrodome to jump to a 2-0 lead in the Series.

When the Series moved to St. Louis for games three, four, and five, it looked as though the sportswriters might have been right after all. The Twins lost all three games. If St. Louis could win just one of the two games back at the Metrodome, they would win the World Series. St. Louis gradually built a 5-2 lead in game six. But the Twins weren't quitting. They rallied with two four-run innings to beat the Cardinals, 11-5. The whole Series would come down to the seventh game.

"The only thing different is we're at home," Kirby said after game six. "We're the best team in baseball at home, and we knew we weren't going to roll over today."

Left fielder Dan Gladden encourages Twins fans to cheer even louder at the Metrodome. The noise distracted some Cardinal players during the World Series.

In the seventh game of the World Series, the Twins capped off the championship with great pitching by Viola and Reardon. Minnesota won the World Series for the first time in the team's 27-year history!

In game six, Kirby had tied two World Series records—for the most times to reach base in one game (five) and for the most runs scored in a game (four).

For his play during the season, he won the Gold Glove and Silver Slugger awards. They are presented to the best defensive player (Gold Glove) and the best offensive player (Silver Slugger) at each position in the league.

Kirby had barely gotten rid of the soreness in his muscles when spring training began in 1988. "I'll take my '87 numbers anytime," he told reporters when they asked him to forecast his performance for the 1988 season. "Why not?" Then, true to his character, he added, "But there's always room for improvement."

Kirby holds up his Silver Slugger Award for fans to see.

In 1988 Kirby and the Twins improved their record. Although the Twins posted a 91-71 record, they finished in second place. The Oakland A's had risen to the top, and they would remain there for three years. But Kirby continued to hit. His .356 average was the highest average for a right-handed batter since Joe DiMaggio hit .357 in 1941.

After the 1988 season, the Twins took a turn for the worse. They went 82-84 in 1989 and ended up in fifth place. Suddenly, baseball was not as much fun. Even so, Kirby tried to keep everyone happy and relaxed with his chatter and teasing. If the clubhouse was quiet, Kirby hadn't arrived. On the field, he hit .339 and won the league batting title.

Kirby decided to try a new way to get on base. He hacked at fewer pitches out of the strike zone. Rather than risk striking out or flying out while swinging away at an inside pitch, Kirby would punch it to right field for a sure single. After all, the Twins needed base runners if they were going to score. The trouble was that no one was hitting Kirby home. He scored only 75 runs in 1989, compared with 109 in 1988 and 96 in 1987. It was the fewest runs he had scored since his rookie year. But day after day, Kirby showed up by 3 P.M. to hit an early round of batting practice. "This year has been really weird for me," Kirby said. "It shows me that no matter how hard you work, this game has a way of humbling you."

The Twins' clubhouse, where players joke and laugh to relax before games, became a more quiet place. Gary Gaetti, who had been a fiery kind of leader on the team, had become a born-again Christian. He was no longer the player who stormed the dugout, stirring the players to the peak of excitement and inspiring them to come from behind and win games. Losing became a heavy burden for everyone, including Kirby.

The 1989 season was frustrating for Kirby and the rest of the Twins.

Jose Canseco (left) and Mark McGwire, known around the league as the Bash Brothers, intimidated opponents with their home-run power.

After each loss, the players filed out of the dugout with their spirits downcast. Kirby often remained on the bench. He sat alone in the far corner of the dugout. He reflected on his performance in the game and questioned himself: Was there anything more I could have done to help us win? He considered the mistakes he made and what he would do differently next time. "You don't want to let people beat you the same way twice," he said.

To make the Twins' situation worse, the Oakland A's, with their giant-sized sluggers—Jose Canseco, Mark McGwire, Dave Parker, and Dave Henderson—intimidated opposing pitchers. The A's became the American League champions and beat the San Francisco Giants in the World Series.

Before the World Series began, Kirby had more important matters than baseball on his mind. His mother died on October 18. "It's just a big emptiness that I won't ever, ever be able to fill again in my life," he said.

He still thinks about his mother every day. "All she ever wanted to teach us was just [to] be responsible," he recalls. "She got the point across to us that Mom and Dad are not going to be around forever, and they wanted us to be able to take care of ourselves." Kirby's values had always been influenced by his parents. Now he knew better than ever what was important to him. "My daddy always said, 'You're going to have more time than money.' I found out now that's not true. You don't know how much time you have," Kirby said. "I grew up without money, so it's no big deal. I've got everything I want. I've got life itself."

Despite his attitude toward money, Kirby would soon have more than he ever thought he might. In late November, he signed a three-year, $9-million contract and became the highest paid player ever in baseball. But the honor was brief. The next day, Rickey Henderson signed an even bigger deal—$12 million for four years. Before long, Kirby's contract looked small compared to what many other superstars were being paid. Kirby seemed to expect the skyrocketing salaries. "Hopefully, this will open up other avenues for other people," Puckett said on the day he signed his contract. "But I'm not going to look over my shoulder. What I've gotten, I'm happy with it."

6

The Last Shall Be First

During spring training in 1990, fortune-tellers of the sports pages predicted doom again for the Twins. That kind of talk bothered Kirby. "I can't stomach those sixth- and seventh-place predictions," he grumbled. But at the end of the season, that's exactly where the Twins had finished — last place. For the first time in a long time, Kirby ended the season hitting below .300 (.298). He hit only 12 home runs. Still, he was selected for the All-Star team for the fifth time.

He was philosophical about his season. "As much as people try to single you out and say you're a superstar," Kirby says, "I try to tell people it's a team game. I can't handle it by myself. I can't pitch, catch, play shortstop, third base. My job is to play center field. Wherever I play, I do my job. Some days you might see me carry the team—five RBI, hit a couple home runs, get a couple hits. That's fine. But it's impossible for me to do it every single day."

Kirby never made excuses. But 1990 had been so dismal a season, he seemed to need to find a reasonable way to look at it. "Some years are going to be better than others," he said, "and you have to understand that. You wish you could win every time. That's what everybody says in spring training.... [W]hat you want to do is win. Things don't always turn out the way you want them to. You just have to keep fighting. To win, believe me, you have to get all the breaks."

Even though he isn't always successful, Kirby gives his best effort each time at bat.

During spring training in 1992, Kirby takes time out from practice to visit with his two favorite fans—wife Tonya and daughter Catherine.

Shortly after the 1990 season ended, Kirby and Tonya adopted a baby girl. They named her Catherine Margaret after both of her grandmothers. To Kirby, she was "the greatest thing that could have happened."

In spring training before the 1991 season, Kirby was already a little tired from being a dad. He had always enjoyed reading during the winter. Now he spent time changing diapers and feeding Catherine. She woke up every day at 5:30 A.M. Kirby got up with her, since during the season he would be gone often, and Tonya would have the job of caring for Catherine all by herself. Kirby loves kids. And spending time with his daughter is important to him because his dad had to work so many hours of the day. "I want to be around my kids all the time," Kirby says. "I want to be there when they're going through all their little tough times so they can come to me."

Kirby and Tonya try to help kids who are in need. In honor of his mother and father, who both died of heart disease, they established the Children's Heart Fund. In 1991 Kirby held the first annual 8-Ball Invitational Billiards Tournament to raise money for the Children's Heart Fund. Among the participants were Bobby Bonilla, who plays for the New York Mets, Cal Ripken, Jr., of the Baltimore Orioles, and two of Kirby's teammates, Chuck Knoblauch and Chili Davis.

The Pucketts also became active in Grand Slam, a program created to bring the anti-drug, anti-alcohol message to kids. "I saw kids ruin their lives when I was a kid," he says. "I saw kids be killed and stabbed. But that's part of life, and I just had to deal with it."

He realizes that, to many kids, he is a hero. That honor makes him uneasy. "I tell kids every day that when you idolize somebody, you should idolize somebody like the president," he explains. "You shouldn't idolize me. I think kids have a hard time thinking that I'm a human being just like them. They look at Kirby Puckett like Kirby Puckett is God. They don't even realize that I'm not even close. I wish I was."

Kirby and Tonya realize that Catherine will have a life full of opportunities they never had. "My kids are going to have it better than I ever did," Kirby says.

Playing billiards not only helps Kirby relax, but it also provides him with a means to raise money for charity. The annual billiards tournament benefits the Children's Heart Fund.

But he also believes that he had everything that is important. "My mom and dad gave me all they could," he says. "I was never cold. We had plenty of food. I'm sure there were a lot more people better off than we were, but I just loved what I had. A lot of guys have said they'd love to be rich. Not me. Some rich people don't teach their kids values. I don't want that for my kids. I want them to be responsible, to make their own friends, and to enjoy life."

Even though Kirby was a tired dad during spring training in 1991, he was in the batting cage working. His work habits are as consistent as the presence of the diamond-studded number 34 that he has worn around his neck since his early years in the league. "Some things are too good to change," he says.

The Twins had gone 74-88 in 1990 and finished in last place. That was nothing new. They had experienced other seasons full of losing. But because they had won the World Series in 1987, losing was harder to take this time. They remembered how good it felt to pull together for a win. They knew how it felt to help each other through the tough times (even a season filled with wins has its difficulties) and then go on and win again. But in 1990, losing tore the Twins apart. They never wanted to experience that again.

There were many new players in camp. Rookie Chuck Knoblauch was competing for the job at second base. Jack Morris, Chili Davis, and Mike Pagliarulo signed with the Twins as free agents from other teams. Rookie Scott Leius made the team during the last week of spring training. After seven years in the majors, Kirby continued to practice hitting the inside pitch over the left-field fence. Kirby had become an example to his teammates, old and new. He worked hard. His attitude was upbeat, no matter what.

Money was a hot topic in 1991. Rickey Henderson wanted to renegotiate his $12-million contract. Several players had signed new contracts and were now making more money than he was. Henderson thought his contract was unfair. Because Kirby refused to ask the Twins to renegotiate his contract, he became a hero to some people. To him, honoring a contract was part of being responsible. He had a job to do.

The Twins had a great spring training, but as soon as the season began, they dug themselves into a hole. By April 20, the Twins were in last place in the American League West.

But gradually the Twins turned things around. A 15-game winning streak helped. On June 1, when the streak began, they were in fifth place with a 23-25 record. By June 16, they were in first place. After July 11 they held first place for the rest of the season. Defeating the Toronto Blue Jays in the American League Championship Series, they won the chance to play in the World Series for the second time in five seasons.

With Kirby's help, especially in game six, the Twins

Kirby celebrates the Twins' 1991 World Series victory by leaping into the arms of pitcher Jack Morris. Morris pitched 10 shutout innings before the Twins scored a run to win the game.

went on to win the 1991 World Series. This time, the sportswriters called it the "Worst-to-First" Series because both teams, Minnesota and Atlanta, had finished last in their divisions the year before.

After game seven, Kirby sat in front of his locker, exhausted. Beside him was Shane Mack, who has sought advice from Kirby ever since Shane joined the Twins in 1990. Shane had struggled through a troublesome World Series. He went 0 for 17 before his first hit, and manager Tom Kelly benched him in game five. Kirby tried to help Shane out of his slump. "I just tried to tell him, 'Don't worry about things you

Kirby and outfielder Shane Mack

can't control,'" Kirby said. "It's common sense. I told him he can't be nobody but who he is. It worked. Yesterday [in game six] he went out there and he swung the bat great." Mack had two hits and drove in a run in game six.

"One more year?" Shane asked Kirby as the two lingered in the clubhouse after the World Series. He hoped to rely on Kirby's help for another year.

"No," said Kirby. "You've been under my wing for two years now. Like when I was a kid, my dad said, 'I want you to grow up to be a man.' I got [to be] 18 and they sent me off to college. I haven't been home since."

All during the 1992 season, Minnesota fans worried that their star outfielder might be playing his last season as a Twin. His contract would run out at the end of the season, making him a free agent. Then he could sign with any team he wanted. In the meantime, Kirby had a fantastic season. He hit the first two grand slams of his career, had more than 200 hits in a season for the fifth time, and batted .329 for the year. He received the second-most votes for the American League MVP Award, behind Oakland closer Dennis Eckersley. His superb season on the field was matched by a happy event off the field. Kirby and Tonya adopted a four-month-old boy in February 1993. They named their son Kirby Puckett, Jr. Despite the weight of the name, Kirby says, "I want him to grow up to be whatever he wants to be."

Throughout the season, fans showed their appreciation for Kirby at home games by standing and cheering nearly every good play the center fielder made. Finally, in December 1992, the Twins signed Kirby to a new contract—for $30 million over five years. Newspapers reported that Kirby could have received contract offers for more money elsewhere, but that he chose to stay and play in Minnesota. At a press conference announcing his new contract, Kirby expressed his joy at returning. "I've played with the Minnesota Twins for nine years, and I couldn't be happier than I am now," he said.

KIRBY PUCKETT'S
BASEBALL STATISTICS

College and Minor Leagues

Year	Team	Games	At Bats	Runs	Hits	Home Runs	RBI	Batting Average	Stolen Bases
1981	Bradley University	53	156	40	59	8	41	.378	21
1982	Triton Junior College	69	254	90	120	16	78	.472	42
1982	Elizabethton (A)	65	275	65	105	3	35	.382	43
1983	Visalia (A)	138	548	105	172	9	97	.314	48
1984	Toledo (AAA)	21	80	9	21	1	5	.263	8

Minor League Highlights:

Region IV Junior College Player of the Year, 1982.
Appalachian League All-Star Team, 1982.
California League All-Star Team, 1983.
California League Player of the Year, 1983.

Major Leagues

Year	Team	Games	At Bats	Runs	Hits	Home Runs	RBI	Batting Average	Stolen Bases
1984	Minnesota	128	557	63	165	0	31	.296	14
1985	Minnesota	161	691	80	199	4	74	.288	21
1986	Minnesota	161	680	119	223	31	96	.328	20
1987	Minnesota	157	624	96	207	28	99	.332	12
1988	Minnesota	158	657	109	234	24	121	.356	6
1989	Minnesota	159	635	75	215	9	85	.339	11
1990	Minnesota	146	551	82	164	12	80	.298	5
1991	Minnesota	152	611	92	195	15	89	.319	11
1992	Minnesota	160	639	104	210	19	110	.329	17
Totals (regular season)		1,382	5,645	820	1,812	142	785	.321	117

Major League Highlights:

Topps Major League All-Rookie Team, 1984.
All-Star Game, 1986, 1987, 1988, 1989, 1990, 1991, 1992.
Rawlings Gold Glove Award, 1986, 1987, 1988, 1989, 1991, 1992.
Silver Slugger Award, 1986, 1987, 1988, 1989.
American League Batting Title, 1989.
American League Championship Series Most Valuable Player, 1991.